LA MALINCHE
INDIGENOUS TRANSLATOR FOR HERNÁN CORTÉS IN MEXICO

WOMEN WHO CHANGED HISTORY

LA MALINCHE
INDIGENOUS TRANSLATOR FOR HERNÁN CORTÉS IN MEXICO

LAURA LORIA

IN ASSOCIATION WITH

Published in 2018 by Britannica Educational Publishing (a trademark of Encyclopædia Britannica, Inc.) in association with The Rosen Publishing Group, Inc.
29 East 21st Street, New York, NY 10010

Copyright © 2018 The Rosen Publishing Group, Inc. and Encyclopædia Britannica, Inc. Encyclopædia Britannica, Britannica, and the Thistle logo are registered trademarks of Encyclopædia Britannica, Inc. All rights reserved.

Distributed exclusively by Rosen Publishing.
To see additional Britannica Educational Publishing titles, go to rosenpublishing.com.

First Edition

Britannica Educational Publishing
J.E. Luebering: Executive Director, Core Editorial
Andrea R. Field: Managing Editor, Compton's by Britannica

Rosen Publishing
Heather Moore Niver: Editor
Nelson Sá: Art Director
Michael Moy: Designer
Cindy Reiman: Photography Manager
Heather Moore Niver: Photo Researcher

Library of Congress Cataloging-in-Publication Data

Names: Loria, Laura, author.
Title: La Malinche : indigenous translator for Hernán Cortés in Mexico / Laura Loria.
Description: First edition. | New York : Britannica Educational Publishing, in association with Rosen Educational Services, [2018] | Series: Women who changed history | Includes bibliographical references and index.
Identifiers: LCCN 2016057947| ISBN 9781680486513 (library bound : alk. paper) | ISBN 9781680486490 (pbk. : alk. paper) | ISBN 9781680486506 (6-pack : alk. paper)
Subjects: LCSH: Marina, approximately 1505-approximately 1530—Juvenile literature. | Mexico—History—Conquest, 1519-1540—Juvenile literature. | Aztec women—Biography—Juvenile literature. | Translators—Mexico—Biography—Juvenile literature. | Indians of Mexico—Biography—Juvenile literature. | Cortés, Hernán, 1485-1547—Juvenile literature.
Classification: LCC F1230.M373 L67 2018 | DDC 972.02092 [B] —dc23
LC record available at https://lccn.loc.gov/2016057947

Manufactured in the United States of America

Photo credits: Cover, pp. 10, 14, 21 PHAS/Universal Images Group/Getty Images; p. 7 Phoenix Art Museum, Arizona, USA/Museum purchase with funds provided by the Friends of Mexican Art/Bridgeman Images; p. 13 v0v/iStock/Thinkstock; p. 15 Photos.com/Thinkstock; p. 16 © Maryann Groves/North Wind Picture Archives; p. 19 Chris Hellier/Alamy Stock Photo; pp. 22–23 Ned M. Seidler/NATIONAL GEOGRAPHIC IMAGE COLLECTION/Getty Images; p. 26 Bettmann/Getty Images; p. 27 Chronicle/Alamy Stock Photo; pp. 28–29, 44 Private Collection /Archives Charmet/Bridgeman Images; pp. 30–31 John Gress/Corbis News/Getty Images; p. 34 Biblioteca Medicea-Laurenziana, Florence, Italy/Bridgeman Images; p. 37 Museo Nacional de Arte, Mexico City, Mexico/Bridgeman Images; p. 39 Mireille Vautier/Alamy Stock Photo; pp. 40–41 Mary Evans Picture Library/Alamy Stock Photo; p. 43 Lucio Ruiz Pastor/age footstock/SuperStock.

CONTENTS

INTRODUCTION   6

CHAPTER ONE
MALINTZIN: FROM WEALTH TO SLAVERY   9

CHAPTER TWO
DOÑA MARINA: CORTÉS' RISING STAR   18

CHAPTER THREE
CONQUERING MEXICO   26

CHAPTER FOUR
THE LEGACY AND MYTH OF LA MALINCHE   36

GLOSSARY   45

FOR FURTHER READING   46

INDEX   47

INTRODUCTION

Think about all of the history you have learned so far. Who were the people you read about? Who did your teachers discuss the most? Most likely, you have learned a history of men and their actions. Men have dominated government, literature, science, and exploration for most of written history. Because women make up about half the people on the planet, why don't we learn more about them?

Of course, there have been some exceptional women in history as well. When you've learned about a woman, it has been because she has accomplished something extraordinary, like the queens Cleopatra of Egypt and Elizabeth I of England. Still, women's stories are often told in the context of the men they were linked to, by blood or marriage.

This seems unfair, but we must consider what the lives of women have been like throughout history. Women have been seen as weak, unintelligent, and too emotional to do anything important in the world. Girls were kept home until they married. Girls from poor families might never even learn to read, while wealthier girls would get a "feminine" education, of reading, writing, simple math, and domestic subjects.

Until the last century, women were expected to stay in the home, cooking and cleaning while raising children. Failing to marry turned a woman into an "old maid" who was pitied. If a woman did work outside the home, usually it was in one of a few occupations deemed suitable for women: servant, teacher, nurse, or factory laborer.

INTRODUCTION 7

Artists can only imagine what the real Malinche looked like. This modern portrait of her may have been based on another Mexican woman.

Malinche's story is unlike most women's of her time. She was able to do things forbidden to most women, like travel, explore, and speak with important leaders. The support of a powerful man, Hernán Cortés, the Spanish conqueror of Mexico, enabled her to do this. Their partnership resulted in the complete takeover of Mexico by the Spanish. Cortés could not have achieved his goals without her knowledge and assistance.

Malinche can be compared to Pocahontas in America. She was a native Mexican Indian who guided a foreigner in her land. She translated for Cortés, not only the local languages, but also the meanings behind the words. It is said that she was always by Cortés' side, and she was certainly of great importance to his mission. It is possible that he would not have succeeded so quickly without her.

Also like Pocahontas, most of the story of Malinche's life is uncertain, or has become something of a myth. None of her writings, if there were any, have survived. She is only briefly mentioned in other historical documents, including those of Cortés. Most of what we know about Malinche was passed down orally, and changed over time.

Unlike Pocahontas, who is seen in a positive light by most Americans, Malinche is a controversial figure among Mexicans. Some see her as a heroine who tried to make the colonization of Mexico as peaceful as possible. Others think she is a traitor to native Mexicans, who sold out her people to save her own life. Perhaps there is some truth to both viewpoints. Her story is fascinating and unusual, like those of most women who changed history.

CHAPTER ONE

MALINTZIN: FROM WEALTH TO SLAVERY

Around the year 1501, a girl named Malintzin was born in the village of Painalla in the Coatzacualco province, located on the Yucatan Peninsula of present-day Mexico. Her father was a cacique, a wealthy and influential man of the Nahua peoples, which included the Aztecs. This group was very powerful and had a large empire. The Aztecs had organized governments and religion, social classes, and a trading economy. They also kept excellent written records.

EARLY LIFE

Although historians don't know a lot about Malintzin, or Malinche, as she came to be widely known, we can guess what her early life was like by looking at the lives of other people in the upper class. As the daughter of a noble, Malinche would have worn clothes of cotton, a fine fabric at the time. She would have had a variety of foods to eat, beyond the local corn and beans, because her family could afford imported food. Her home would have been made

As a daughter of a wealthy man, Malinche would have been used to wearing fine clothes. It is likely that she dressed that way with Cortés.

MALINTZIN: FROM WEALTH TO SLAVERY

THE MANY NAMES OF MALINCHE

The woman we call Malinche has been called many different names. Some of this is the result of mistranslations or mispronunciation by non-native speakers. Her birth name was Malinali. The formal version of this name, which would be used by the native peoples of Mexico, was Malintzin.

The Spanish invaders, who did not have an ear for her language, misheard it as Malinche. (She was later also referred to as La Malinche.) The Spaniards gave her the name Marina when she was baptized, because it was a Christian name. Doña was added to it, as a sign of respect. Although she was a slave, she was regarded highly by her captors.

In a twist on gender roles, the native Mexicans often referred to Hernán Cortés as "El Malinche," or Lord Malinche, as if he had taken her name.

out of stone and contain many rooms. Her family's wealth allowed them to have servants, so she could spend her time getting some education, rather than doing chores at home. Aztec children were taught to be polite, respectful, honest, and to have self-control. They should always be well behaved.

Tragedy struck her family when she was young. Her father died, and her mother remarried soon after. At this time, a woman needed a husband to protect and support her family. She had a son with her new husband. Because she wanted her son to inherit the wealth left behind by Malinche's father, she had to find a way to get rid of her daughter. This sounds cruel, but people at that time had a different view of the importance of children.

In many cultures, the birth of a girl was not as important as the birth of a boy. Boys could provide labor, on a farm or in another job that would help the household survive. If the father of the family died, an older boy could support the women and children left behind. When the boy became a man, he would inherit the family business or farm, and marry and have children of his own, who would carry on his name. In short, a boy was a gift to his family, while a girl was a burden.

According to legend, Malinche's mother had a servant whose daughter had died. Malinche's mother pretended that it was her own daughter, buried her, and soon spread the word that Malinche had died. In reality, Malinche was sold into slavery, which was a common practice. She was about eight or nine years old. Now, her stepbrother could inherit everything when he grew up.

MOVING ON

In secret, Malinche was sent to a family in Xicalango. She probably assumed that she would never see her family again. She was probably frightened, confused, and angry about what had happened to her. Because she had been a person of high social status, adjusting to the life of a

MALINTZIN: FROM WEALTH TO SLAVERY | 13

WHO WERE THE AZTECS?

The Aztec people were the rulers of Mexico in the fifteenth and early sixteenth centuries, until the Spanish conquered them. Their capital city, Tenochtitlán, had beautiful palaces and temples, and was extremely wealthy. They kept written records of their gods and events, used a calendar, and traded using a barter system, throughout their land. They did not invent many new things, but incorporated the discoveries of the civilizations that came before them.

Their empire was widespread, but not managed well by the emperor Montezuma II. Many tribes in the empire rebelled against Aztec rule and there was constant fighting. This weakness made it easier for the Spanish to take over.

The Aztec people adapted the Mayan calendar, which combines three calendars in a circular pattern to mark one year.

LA MALINCHE

A Tabascan leader gave Malinche, along with nineteen other women, to Cortés as a gift of surrender.

MALINTZIN: FROM WEALTH TO SLAVERY

slave must have been incredibly difficult. She was not used to hard work.

She did not stay in Xicalango for very long. Malinche was soon traded to the cacique, or leader, of the Tabasco region. After several years, in March of 1519, the Chontal people of Tabasco went to war with the invading Spanish forces, led by Hernán Cortés. Malinche would have been a teenager at this time. The Chontal were defeated easily by the Spanish, with their advanced weapons. They surrendered, offering Malinche and nineteen other slaves as a peace offering. Once again, Malinche was taken against her will.

MEETING CORTÉS

When the Spanish accepted Malinche and the other slaves, they were immediately baptized as Catholics and taught about their new faith. They were the first women baptized in the Americas, according to Bernal Díaz del Castillo, a Spanish soldier and writer who accompanied Cortés to Mexico. No one asked them if they wanted to become

Hernán Cortés conquered Mexico for Spain in the early 1500s, with the help of native allies and advisors, like Malinche.

16 | LA MALINCHE

Malinche was described as very beautiful, but there is nothing else written about her appearance.

Christians—this was to become standard practice for the conquerors.

Cortés assigned the young women to several of his men. Malinche stood out, because of her beauty and regal manners. She was described by Díaz as "a very excellent person" because of her unique qualities. Cortés gave her to his friend Alonso Hernández Puertocarrero, who renamed her Marina. She must have stayed on Cortés' mind, though. He soon sent Puertocarrero back to Spain, and took Malinche for himself.

CHAPTER TWO

DOÑA MARINA: CORTÉS' RISING STAR

Malinche, called Doña Marina by the Spanish, was in an unusual position. She was a slave, so she had no say in her destiny, but an extremely powerful man was attracted to her. She must have felt conflicted, because although Cortés was trying to defeat her people, he was also kind to her. Malinche had a chance to influence him and his course of action.

One of Malinche's greatest strengths was her ability to learn new languages. Her first language was Nahuatl, but when she was enslaved in Tabasco, she learned two more languages, which were Mayan dialects. This is how she first distinguished herself from the other slave women.

HIDDEN TALENTS

Legend says that Father Jerónimo de Aguilar, a Spanish priest who had lived as a captive with some Mexican Indians, discovered her talent for language. According to the

DOÑA MARINA: CORTÉS' RISING STAR | 19

Malinche was said to have always been by Cortés' side, translating both words and meaning for him.

SLAVERY IN EARLY MEXICO

The word "slave," for most people, is associated with the African slave trade by Europeans and Americans. However, slavery has been a part of nearly all cultures across the globe. Most slaves in history were local people who were conquered by another group and used for free labor. In early American and Mexican history, the Europeans who came over enslaved many Indians.

It was common for Native Americans to be sent back to Europe as slaves. When the diseases the Europeans brought over began to reduce the population of the Indians, the import of African slaves became more common.

In 1542 the Spanish rulers of Mexico issued the *Leyes Nuevas*, or "New Laws," which limited the Spaniards' use of natives for labor. These laws provided at least some protection for the Indians, but in many Spanish colonies, the laws were often ignored.

story, Aguilar overheard her talking to some native women. Because he had spent much time in the area among the native people, he recognized that she was speaking in Nahuatl, not the Mayan he had heard her speak before. Another story says that Malinche's talent was discovered when representatives of Montezuma, the Aztec emperor, came to visit. Father Aguilar was embarrassed when he was unable to communicate with them. Malinche, who had been listening, pointed to Cortés after the visitors had

DOÑA MARINA: CORTÉS' RISING STAR

Father Jerónimo de Aguilar is credited with bringing Malinche's special skills to Cortés' attention.

22 | LA MALINCHE

The legend of Malinche's intervention during this meeting with Montezuma's people shows how critical her presence was for Cortés' success.

asked a question. They immediately bowed to him, which showed that she had understood that they were asking who the leader was.

This discovery made Malinche a particularly valuable person to have on hand, as she could communicate with more people than he could. Because she could speak Mayan and Nahuatl, and Aguilar could speak both Mayan

DOÑA MARINA: CORTÉS' RISING STAR

and Spanish, together they could communicate with many people. Aguilar began to tutor Malinche in Spanish. She learned quickly—some say it only took four months. Bernal Díaz wrote that "without the help of doña Marina we could not have understood the language of New Spain and Mexico." He also wrote that, when she began to translate for the Spanish, they had truly begun their conquest.

RIGHT-HAND WOMAN

Her value was immediately apparent to Cortés, who quickly regretted giving her to a colleague. Many historians have written that Cortés sent Puertocarrero, her first Spanish master, away just to take Malinche back. Their relationship was unusual. Very few slave women had such a close relationship with their masters, and even fewer were held in such high regard.

For Malinche, this closeness to Cortés was like walking a tightrope. She wanted to stay in his favor, because her very life depended on it. The Tabascans had killed another of his translators after Cortés defeated them in a battle. She was torn between the two sides of this conflict. Malinche would have to consider every move she made with extreme care.

A translator can explain what words mean in different languages, but Malinche was much more than just a translator. Having been born into a wealthy family, she was familiar with the customs and manners of the upper classes. These were the types of people who Cortés dealt with. If he could follow their social rules, they would be less afraid of him, and perhaps negotiations would be easier. By following Malinche's lead in manners and customs, Cortés had an advantage over the native Mexicans.

After her transition into slave life, Malinche was also exposed to many different cultures. Unlike most women, who lived their whole lives in the home, Malinche had traveled and mixed with different people. With this knowledge, she could advise Cortés on how to speak with different people. She knew how they thought.

She was also familiar with the religious beliefs of the native people. To Christians like the Spanish, the native Mexicans' beliefs seemed strange and superstitious. Cortés could use that information to manipulate the people into doing what he wanted. If he could convince the people that their gods wanted him to take over the land, they would surrender out of fear that the gods would punish them. Malinche could give him this insight into their culture.

A CLOSE RELATIONSHIP

Cortés and Malinche had a personal relationship as well. Although married, Cortés, like many other conquistadores, did not bring his wife to Mexico. It was common for the Spanish invaders to have relationships with their slaves. The slaves, of course, had no choice in the matter.

As a result of their relationship, Malinche became pregnant with his child. In 1522, three years after she became his captive, she gave birth to his son. She named him Martín Cortés, showing that although she was not married to Cortés, he was the boy's father. He is recognized as the first mestizo, or mixed-race person, born in Mexico, because of his Spanish and Indian heritage. Of course, it is likely that other children of mixed descent were born before Martín, but the legend persists.

CHAPTER THREE

CONQUERING MEXICO

Malinche did not just stand by Cortés' side, helping him as he took action. She also, at his urging, acted as a spy, an orator, and a negotiator in her own right. Her personal accomplishments are astonishing for any woman, let alone a native slave girl in occupied territory. However, historians have challenged many of the tales of her deeds. They are considered legends, as there is little proof that they really happened as the stories say.

DOUBLE AGENT

One tribe that Cortés found particularly difficult to defeat was the Tlaxcalans. Although they were not loyal to the emperor, Montezuma,

Malinche's presence at official meetings may have reassured the native Mexicans that cooperating with Cortés was the right thing to do.

CONQUERING MEXICO | 27

they were also not eager to be taken over by a foreign power. Frustrated and unsure of what to do, Cortés asked Malinche to find out what the people were saying.

According to this story, an older woman of high rank befriended Malinche. The woman begged her to leave her captor, to save herself. She told Malinche that Montezuma's army was planning to massacre the Spanish, and that Malinche would suffer the same fate if she

When Cortés was unable to conquer the Tlaxcalans, he asked Malinche to gather information. She learned about plans for an attack on Cortés, which allowed him to strike first.

stayed with them. She said that her husband, a cacique like Malinche's father, had told her so.

It must have been tempting for Malinche to do just that: abandon Cortés and return to her own people. The woman even promised that Malinche could marry her son, escaping slavery and living a life of comfort. Malinche resolved to stay with Cortés, but she didn't tell the woman that.

Accepting the woman's offer, Malinche said that she would steal away back to her camp, to get her things. Instead, she ran to tell Cortés immediately. When he confirmed that what she told him was true, he attacked the Aztec army before they could attack him. The Spanish were successful, killing three thousand men in the battle.

WOMAN OF FAITH

Cortés was appalled by the religious beliefs and practices of the Aztecs, particularly human sacrifice. He found it barbaric, and the thought

CONQUERING MEXICO | 29

As a Christian, Cortés found the religious practices of the Aztecs strange. Malinche helped him to understand them, and use them to his advantage. In this illustration he burns their idols.

30 | LA MALINCHE

Cortés aimed to steer the native people away from their worship of Quetzalcoátal, shown as a serpent, and toward the Christian God.

CONQUERING MEXICO 31

of becoming one of their human sacrifices terrified him. In turn, he tried to scare them with his loud weapons. He thought the Aztecs believed that he and his men were gods, so at least initially, he was careful to make sure they never saw the corpse of a Spanish soldier.

In fact, some of the native people believed that the god Quetzalcoátal might have sent him. That theory was surely disproven when he set out to destroy their temples, which he felt were sacrilegious. Many European conquerors justified taking over native people and their territories by claiming that they were there to save their souls. The spread of Christianity around the world was only part of their goal.

They really wanted wealth and power. Religion was just a convenient excuse.

While Malinche was forced to convert by her captor, Bernal Díaz wrote of her love of the faith. He describes a time when she met with her birth family and told them the biblical story of Joseph from the Old Testament, in which Joseph ultimately reconciled with his family even though his brothers had once sold him into slavery in Egypt. The historical record shows that this was a bit of fiction, however. Malinche did not reunite with her family until many

AZTEC RITUALS

The Aztec worshiped a host of gods who personified the forces of nature. To obtain the gods' aid, the worshipers performed penances and took part in innumerable elaborate rituals and ceremonies. Human sacrifice played an important part in the rites. Because life was man's most precious possession, the Aztec reasoned, it was the most acceptable gift for the gods. As the Aztec nation grew powerful, more and more sacrifices were needed to keep the favor of the gods. At the dedication of the great pyramid temple in Tenochtitlán, twenty thousand captives were killed. They were led up the steps of the high pyramid to the altar, where chiefs and priests took turns at slitting open their bodies and tearing out their hearts. While we do not know if Malinche herself ever took part in these rituals, they were a part of her culture.

years later, shortly before she died, and that meeting was not described in any known documents.

Despite her forced conversion to Christianity, she actively participated in its spread. Malinche would have had to translate baptism ceremonies for the native Mexicans. She convinced many Aztecs to convert, preaching about her faith to people in their own language. Surely, this was more effective than having a Spanish person try to convince the native Mexicans to give up their religious rituals.

POWERS OF PERSUASION

The emperor of the Aztec empire, Montezuma, was astounded by Cortés' many victories. In an attempt to kill the Spanish invaders, he invited them to Tenochtitlán for a supposedly peaceful meeting. He planned to attack them. When Cortés found out, he angrily confronted Montezuma.

Thankfully, Malinche was there to keep things calm. She allegedly convinced Montezuma that he would never defeat the Spanish. She told him that he must give himself up to the Spanish army, and live with them. He was allowed to continue ruling while he was held captive. According to this story, a slave girl had managed to convince an emperor to give up his empire.

It didn't happen overnight. During months of his imprisonment, Montezuma sabotaged his own people's attempts at driving the Spanish out of Tenochtitlán. Tensions grew between the warring sides. Montezuma's submission to

34 | LA MALINCHE

Malinche allegedly managed to convince Montezuma to surrender to Cortés, which led to Spain's eventual victory in Mexico.

the Spaniards eroded the respect of his people. According to Spanish accounts, he attempted to speak to his subjects and was assailed with stones and arrows, suffering wounds from which he died three days later. The Aztecs, however, believed the Spaniards had murdered their emperor, and Cortés' force was nearly destroyed as it tried to sneak out of Tenochtitlán at night. Cortés and Malinche were lucky to survive the retreat.

While they were away, the Spanish suffered many more setbacks. All seemed to be lost, until, almost a year after he left Tenochtitlán, Cortés returned with a reorganized army to take Mexico for good. The Aztecs, starving and weakened by disease, gave up their fight in August 1521, only two years after Cortés began his quest for control of Mexico.

CHAPTER FOUR

THE LEGACY AND MYTH OF LA MALINCHE

After the conquest, and the birth of their son, Malinche and Cortés drifted apart. While he still relied on her translation services, they no longer had a personal relationship. This was a result of several factors. One, Cortés was already married to a Spanish woman, Catalina Suárez Marcayda, so he could not continue a relationship with Malinche. However, his wife died in late 1522, the same year Martín Cortés was born. The real reason he distanced himself from Malinche was that she was a Mexican Indian, and it would not be acceptable for him to marry her in his social circle. The excitement of their time together during the conquest was gone, and Cortés went back to his regular life.

LIFE AFTER CORTÉS

Although he no longer wanted to be with her, he made sure that Malinche and their son were cared for. Cortés arranged

THE LEGACY AND MYTH OF LA MALINCHE | 37

The relationship between Malinche and Cortés ended after the conquest, but he ensured she and their son were taken care of.

a marriage for her to a knight named Juan Jaramillo in 1524. Cortés gave several valuable pieces of Mexican land to the Jaramillos, including one once owned by Montezuma himself.

Malinche and Juan had a daughter named María in 1526. Their marriage was reportedly not particularly happy, but it was uneventful. Malinche may have died as

THE LIFE OF MARTÍN CORTÉS

First, it is important to distinguish which Martín Cortés we are referring to. Hernán Cortés had a habit of giving the same names to different children. He had two sons named Martín, which was also his father's name. The Martín born to Malinche was his first son given the name.

Martín's father took him to Spain when he was six. He never saw his mother again. Martín grew up in luxury as part of the court of Prince Philip (later King Philip II) of Spain and later entered military service. He married and had at least one child, a son. In 1563, he returned to Mexico.

Martín, supporting his younger half-brother Martín's ambition to gain control of Mexico, allegedly became involved in an attempt at a revolution. The elder Martín was arrested for fomenting rebellion; though he denied the charges, he was tortured, imprisoned, and finally sent back to Spain, forbidden to return to Mexico. Few details are known about the remainder of his life, though he may have resumed active military service before his death in about 1569.

early as 1528 or 1529, perhaps having succumbed to a disease brought over by the Europeans, like many native Mexicans. A number of sources, however, indicate that she died around 1550.

MOTHER OF ALL MESTIZOS

During the colonial period, genetic and cultural mixing between Europeans, Africans, and indigenous peoples started almost immediately upon contact, although some elite Europeans disavowed it. The offspring of mixed unions were recognized as socially distinct from their parents, and the term mestizo was coined to refer to people of indigenous and European heritage (while the term mulatto referred to a person of African and European descent). Although it is extremely unlikely that Malinche's son, Martín, was the first

Malinche is represented in many forms of Mexican art, such as this mask used in a traditional dance.

mestizo, Malinche became known as the "Mother of All Mestizos." She represents the blending of two cultures into a new, mixed culture. This is a direct result of the Spanish invasion and conquest of Mexico. It follows that Malinche and Cortés are the symbolic parents of modern Mexico.

LA MALINCHISTA

To some, Malinche represents the evils of colonialism. She is viewed as a traitor to indigenous Mexicans, and a woman who sold them out to save her own neck.

A Spanish word used in Mexico is "malinchista," which means traitor to your country.

It is true that Malinche had a large role in securing Spanish control of her people and their land. Her skills

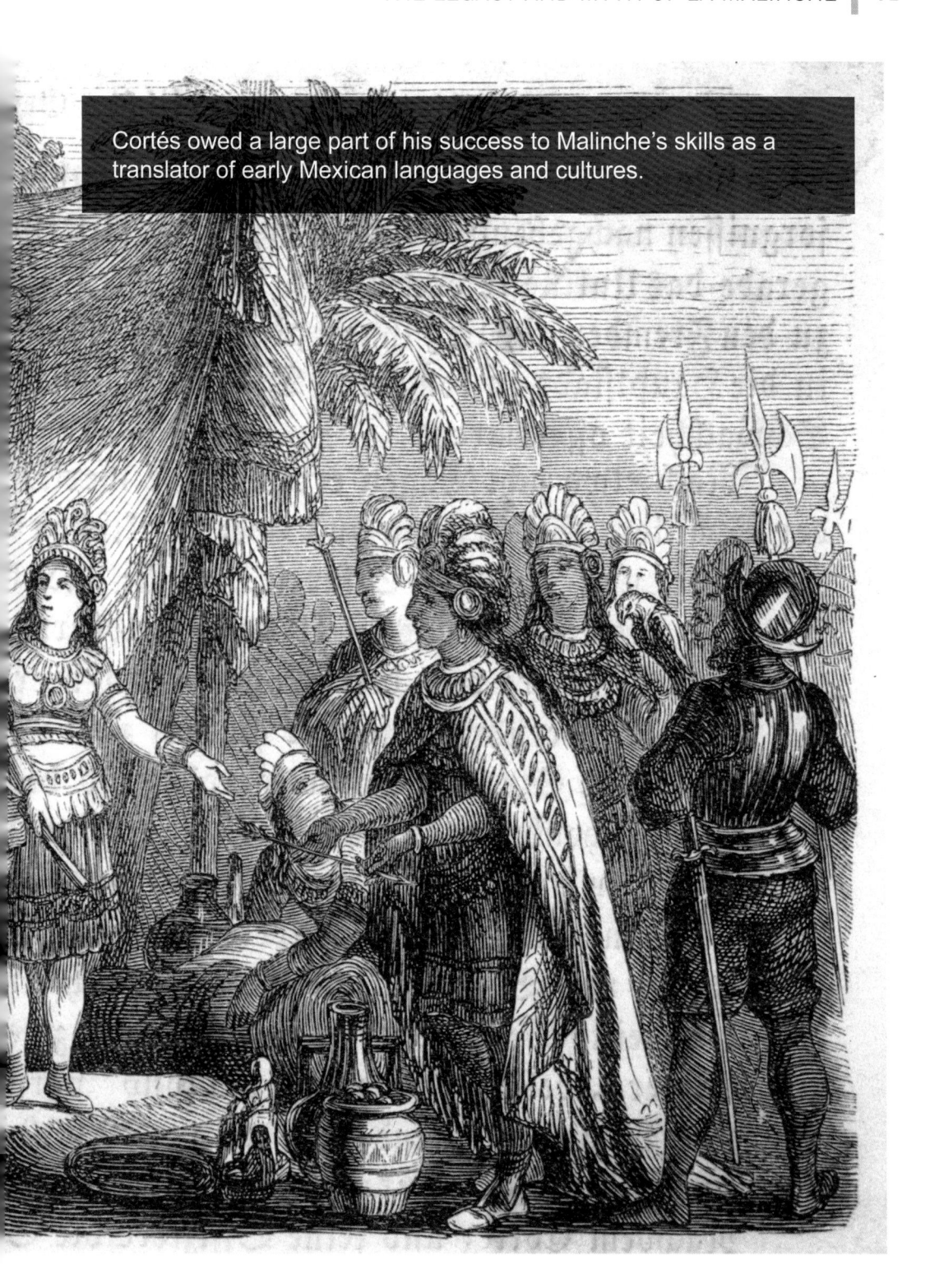

THE LEGACY AND MYTH OF LA MALINCHE 41

Cortés owed a large part of his success to Malinche's skills as a translator of early Mexican languages and cultures.

and talents helped Cortés to conquer Mexico, and thousands of Mexican Indians were killed in the process. If the story of the woman who offers her a chance for escape is true, then Malinche could have left Cortés and joined the native people in their fight against him.

In Mexican art, Malinche is sometimes portrayed like Eve from the Christian Bible. In that story, Eve is responsible for the exile of humans from the earthly paradise of the Garden of Eden. She, like Malinche, is depicted as a wicked figure. Malinche was also an unusual woman for her time. A slave girl was supposed to be quiet, and do only as she was told. Malinche distinguished herself, rose above her station in life, and achieved more than most men. Women who behaved in such a way, against cultural standards, were often despised.

SURVIVOR AND VISIONARY

Malinche's legacy can be viewed in a more positive light. When considered from her perspective, it seems as though Malinche made the best of her situation, and tried to prevent the loss of Mexican life when possible. Yes, she obtained some advantages for herself, but she also suffered greatly for them.

Sold into slavery as a child, Malinche did not have the guidance of a loving parent. She did whatever she could to survive. Perhaps she had seen bad things happen to slaves who were disobedient, and that scared her into submission when she was given to Cortés. Modern psychologists have

THE LEGACY AND MYTH OF LA MALINCHE

Some argue that, while helping the enemy, Malinche did what she thought was best for her people.

identified a phenomenon known as "Stockholm syndrome," which affects hostages. Psychologists say that people who are held captive sometimes begin to identify closely with their captors, as well as with their agenda and demands. Perhaps this is what happened to Malinche.

Another point of view is that Malinche saw the writing on the wall. Maybe she knew that Spanish conquest was inevitable, and so she helped Cortés in an effort to make the transition as painless as possible. In many cases, she convinced people to find peaceful solutions to their conflicts. Malinche used her considerable talent of negotiation, along

Malinche's role in the conquest of Mexico may have saved the lives of many indigenous people.

with her deep understanding of her native culture, to minimize harm for what she knew would happen anyway, the colonization of Mexico.

Malinche's legacy will continue to be debated, studied, and redefined as time goes on and more information about her life is uncovered. As a symbol of her country, she will live forever. Malinche is one of the few women of her time to have a great influence on history.

GLOSSARY

baptized Having received the sacrament of baptism, a religious ritual involving the use of water and marking the entry of a person into a community of believers.
barbaric Savage, primitive, or crude.
cacique A local chief or boss; the term is of Indian origin but was adopted by the Spanish conquistadores to describe heads of Indian tribes.
captor A person who holds another person against his or her will.
colonization The practice of invading a territory and claiming it for your country.
conqueror One who takes over a land and its people by force.
conquistador Spanish for conqueror.
controversial A topic that makes people react strongly.
dialect A local version of a language.
exile To send away and not allow to return.
incorporated Added to something and mixed together.
justified Having a good reason to do something.
legacy Left behind by a person.
massacre The killing of many people at once.
mestizo Spanish term for a person of mixed race.
orator A public speaker.
sabotaged When plans are ruined by another person.
sacrilegious Against a person's religious beliefs.
superstitious Belief that is irrational or that results from trust in magic or fear of the unknown.
traitor A person who betrays someone.

FOR FURTHER READING

Anderson, Zachary. *Hernán Cortés: Conquering the Aztec Empire*. Buffalo, NY: Cavendish Square Publishing, 2015.

Duran, Gloria. *Malinche: Slave Princess of Cortez*. Hamden, CT: Linnet Books, 1993.

Greek, Joe. *Hernán Cortés: Conquistador, Colonizer, and Destroyer of the Aztec Empire*. New York, NY: Rosen Young Adult, 2016.

Green, Carl. *Cortés: Conquering the Powerful Aztec Empire*. New York, NY: Enslow Publishers, 2010.

Mahoney, Emily Jankowski. *Ancient Aztec Culture*. New York, NY: Powerkids Press, 2016.

Niver, Heather Moore. *Ancient Aztec Daily Life*. New York, NY: Powerkids Press, 2016.

Serrano, Francisco. *La Malinche: The Princess Who Helped Cortés Conquer an Empire*. Toronto, ON: Groundwood Books, 2012.

Stuckey, Rachel. *Life Among the Aztec*. New York, NY: Powerkids Press, 2016.

WEBSITES

Because of the changing nature of internet links, Rosen Publishing has developed an online list of websites related to the subject of this book. This site is updated regularly. Please use this link to access this list:

http://www.rosenlinks.com/WWCH/malinche

INDEX

A

Aztec, 9, 11, 13, 20, 28, 31, 33, 35
   rituals, 32

C

cacique, 9, 15, 28
conquerors, 8, 17, 31
conquest of Mexico, 26–35, 42
Cortés, Hernán, 8, 15, 17, 18, 20, 24, 25, 26, 27, 28, 33, 35, 38, 40
   birth of son, 25, 36
   marriage, 36
   relationship with Malinche, 25
Cortés, Martín (son), 25, 36, 38, 39

M

Malinche, 8
   baptized Catholic, 15, 32–33
   birth, 9
   birth of daughter, 38
   birth of son, 25
   daughter of a noble, 9
   death, 38–39
   as double agent, 26–28
   early life, 11–12
   helping Cortés, 24, 26, 33, 43
   learns new languages, 18, 22–23
   legacy, 40, 42–44
   life after Cortés, 36–39
   many names of, 9, 11, 18
   marriage, 38
   meeting Cortés, 15, 17
   parents of, 9, 11, 12, 32–33
   relationship with Cortés, 25
   as slave, 15, 17, 18, 42
   sold into slavery, 12
   as teen, 15
   as translator, 24
mestizo, 25, 39, 40
Montezuma, 13, 20, 26, 27, 33, 35, 38

P

Pocahontas, 8

Q

Quetzalcoátal, 31

R

religious beliefs, 25, 28, 31, 32, 33

S

slavery in early Mexico, 20

W

women in history, 6